Trading Habits

39 of the World's Most

Powerful Stock Market Rules

By Steve Burns & Holly Burns

Contents

When did I start trading?

Looking back at my life, I don't remember a time when I was not interested in the markets. As a teen, I was fascinated by compound return tables, and the magic of growing capital over time. Before the Internet, I remember looking at stock quotes in the newspaper, and my love for trading and the markets has only continued to grow.

I have spent the last 20+ years investing and trading. My drive to be a successful trader lead to reading hundreds of trading books and putting what I learned into action. Because the learning curve was so steep, I decided to create a shortcut for new traders; the kind of information I wish I could have studied when I was getting started. The New Trader 101 e-course and trading book is that shortcut. I have condensed all the key principles that a new trader needs to know into an easily understandable format. My goal is to get a new trader up to speed quickly, and trading successfully, with very little risk.

I hope you will join me as I show you how to build and grow your own capital, with low stress and minimal risk. It will most likely be one of the most rewarding things you ever do. It was for me.

-Steve Burns
www.NewTraderU.com
@sjosephburns

The Power of Habits

"The right trading behaviors start as rules and evolve into habits."
– Brett Steenbarger

In athletics, business, and entertainment, the top performers are those that carefully consider every action they take. The elite have trained themselves to be nimble; habitually doing the right thing, at the right moment. Their years of study and practice have taught their mind and body to react without hesitation, regardless of pressure or uncertainty.

When first studying a winning technique, the process is mechanical and thoughtful. "Do A, then B, and you will likely arrive at C". Speed in action comes from knowing exactly what to do on a deeper, subconscious level. Once you know the right move to make, the final step is to commit to a regimen of dedicated practice. Only then will you be able to outperform your opponents.

In trading, the first step is to learn what you need to do in order to be profitable. Education should be your first priority. Nurturing your comprehension of trading vocabulary is critical to your success. Trading methods, trading systems, trading plans, risk/reward ratios, and win rates can sound mysterious to newcomers. Find good sources of trading information and learn as much as you can.

Continued learning through chart studies, backtesting price patterns, interacting with experienced traders, and reading great trading material are some of the best habits a new trader can develop.

Always focus on being better today than you were yesterday.

Another way to gain an advantage over your opponents is to trade with discipline. Most traders are trading based on their own predictions, opinions, and emotions. These make the worst trading signals. Instead, develop trading rules that will guide you. Replace your opinions with trade signals, your ego with position sizing, and your emotions with a trading plan.

When you have the right set of rules and follow them long enough, they will slowly become part of your trading personality and style and you will follow them on a subconscious level. You will know that you have reached trading maturity when it becomes uncomfortable to break your trading rules. This signifies that they have become second-nature to you, and they're more powerful than your emotionally driven impulses.

Developing and practicing powerful trading habits has made me successful in the stock market for more than 20 years, and they can help you, too.

Rule 1 - 15

The Foundation

1. A winning trading system must either be designed to have a large winning percentage, or big wins and small losses.

There are two paths to profitable trading, accuracy of winning trades and size of winning trades. A trading system with equal size wins and losses must have more wins than losses. This may seem like common sense, but high win rate systems can quickly become unprofitable when losses are allowed to get out of hand. Many of these systems give losing trades too much room to run, and they achieve their high win rate by holding long enough for the trade to come back to even or become profitable.

High win rate systems no longer work when a market environment changes from range bound to trending, because losing trades don't always bounce back. These systems must be built on the accuracy of an entry and the probability of success, rather than holding and hoping that a losing trade will come back. It is crucial to cut losers short, even in high win rate trading systems, because a large loss doesn't give back a large amount of previously earned profits.

High winning percentage systems have to be built on the odds that the profitable price target is reached, or the trailing stop is hit for a profit before the stop loss is reached. The old Wall Street saying "You can't go broke taking a profit" is not true. If you take only small profits, all it takes is a few big losses to break you.

In contrast, there are systems with less wins than losses, but they are profitable over the long term. Losses are kept small and the winning trades are larger than the losing ones. Lower winning percentage systems are typically used by long term trend followers, breakout traders, and option buyers. The bigger their winning trades, the lower their winning percentage can be to still be profitable.

The key is capping the downside risk when you're wrong, but leaving the upside profit potential open. In other words, cut your losers short, but let your winners run. You can let winning trades trend as far as possible, capturing those unexpected, outsized moves that are outside the bell curve of normal price movement.

To be profitable in a low win rate system, you don't have to be right every time, you just have to right big and wrong small. If you're right, you stay right for as long as possible. If you're wrong, you get out with a small loss and wait for the next opportunity. Cutting winners short at the beginning of a trend and letting a loser run on the wrong side of a trend, are the biggest causes of unprofitability.

1:1 risk/reward ratio requires greater than 50% win rate for profitability.

1:2 risk/reward ratio requires greater than 33% win rate for profitability.

1:3 risk/reward ratio requires greater than 25% win rate for profitability.

1:5 risk/reward ratio requires greater than 17% win rate for profitability.

The bigger your wins, the fewer you need to be profitable. The more accurate your entries and exits, the less losses you will endure. You can be profitable with fewer wins as long as losses are kept small. Large losses are the fastest path to being unprofitable, regardless of circumstances.

2. Your trading system must be built on quantifiable facts and not opinions.

Few new traders graduate from trading opinions and predictions, to trading price action and signals. New traders may take trades based on feelings, but professionals base their trades on fact. A signal is a quantifiable reason to take a trade based on price action, a technical indicator, a trend line, or a price pattern. Even when using psychology of the market to your advantage, you must consider these technical strategies.

"Buying a dip" is not a signal. But buying a pullback in the S & P 500 Index to the 50 day SMA, or the prices reaching the 30 RSI on a daily chart inside an uptrend over the 200 day SMA, is based on quantifiable facts. Signals should be researched on historical charts or backtested to see the profitability of trading off the signal. Historical price patterns tend to repeat themselves, and create tradable signals for capturing trends and reversals.

Other types of signals are more discretionary and can rely on pure price action and buying breakouts of price ranges, trend lines, and chart patterns. Trading breakouts of ranges, lines, and patterns are quantifiable, but they leave a lot of discretion in the hands of the trader, and are difficult to backtest. Traders have to stay consistent with how they draw trend lines, identify chart patterns, and read price action, so they don't start seeing what they want to see.

Breakout trading is trying to capture the beginning of a new trend as price leaves the previous trading range and signals a potential change in trend. Having a reason for taking a trade is still better than trading off a hunch, a belief, a feeling, or a prediction. I personally prefer using more quantified trading signals, like price support and resistance levels, moving averages, MACD, and RSI.

It is important to have a specific reason for entering a trade that will put the odds in your favor. This gives you potential for a good winning percentage, risk/reward ratio, and a great chance to be on the right side of the trend in your time frame. Trading without quantifiable signals means you're trading randomly. Replace your discretionary trading with quantifiable signals that give you a specific reason for entering a trade. Beliefs and predictions about what the market will do, should do, or can't possibly do, is not a trading system. Quantified entries and exits in a tested trading system is the path to profitability.

3. Look for low risk, high reward, and high probability setups. – Richard Weissman

When entering a trade, you want there to be a low probability that your stop loss level will be triggered. If you buy Apple stock when the price is 1% over the 200 day SMA, and Apple has not closed below the 200 day SMA in 18 months, then there is a good chance that your stop loss will not be triggered if you set it as a close under the Apple 200 day SMA. You should have a low risk to your account if your stop loss is hit. Buying 100 shares of Apple at $120 a share in a $100,000 trading account with an end of day stop loss $1.20 away from your entry, is a low risk setup. (Of course it is low risk as long as earnings aren't being released the next day while you're still holding this stock position).

It is a great risk to reward ratio if your price target is a 6% price rally back to the 50 day SMA, or a 10% rally back to uptrend highs. Each entry should have a great stop loss level that has a low risk of being triggered. Your position sizing should have low risk so that in the event of a big loss, you will live to fight another day. Your reward should be two or three times larger than your capital at risk to make the trade worth the risk. This may give you a smaller win, but you should have that potential.

Trade so that when you're wrong your losses are small. Look for trades with the potential of being big winners. Enter when the odds are low that your stop loss will be hit before you're profitable enough to exit. Use trailing stops when possible to maximize winning trades, exit a winner when you have a reason to, and not because open profits make you nervous.

4. The answer to the question, "What's the trend?" is the question, "What's your timeframe? – Richard Weissman

The best way to profit in the stock market, or any financial market, is to capture a trend in your time frame. There are other ways, like selling option premium or hedging production by selling futures contracts. But the majority of market participants are trying to capture a trend on their own trading or investing time frame. Buy and hold investors are betting on the long term uptrend of the stock market over the course of their working life. Day traders try to capture trends from the time the market opens, until the time it closes, all in one day. Swing traders are looking to buy a low and then sell it as it trends higher over a few days, or sell a high price short and cover it at a lower price over a few days'.

I have found that the longer the time frame, the simpler it is to capture the trend. Long term trend followers filter out the noise and capture trends on daily or weekly charts, and strive to avoid the random, intra-day noise. Different systems will work based on the velocity and volatility of the trend in a particular time frame.

In a strongly trending market that consistently makes higher highs and higher lows each day for weeks at a time, trend followers do well. Markets that stay inside a defined range of resistance and support on the daily chart for weeks, will prove profitable for swing traders. Day traders like intra-day volatility, as it gives them chances to be profitable.

Any trading system on any time frame is just a set of rules that give the trader a high probability to capture a trend. When building a trading system and developing a trading plan, your goal is to discover ways to capture trends in a way that makes you comfortable psychologically and financially profitable.

5. Start with the weekly price chart to establish the long term trend, and then work down through the daily and hourly charts to trade in the direction of that trend. The odds are better if you're trading in the direction of the long term trend.

Trends are created on the long term charts by the accumulation or distribution of a stock, commodity, or even a whole asset class. During the time an asset is being accumulated, buyers are purchasing and then holding that asset, removing much of the downward selling pressure from that market. The higher highs and higher lows on the chart will show this. It takes higher prices to buy-in, because the current holders of the asset aren't selling and have removed the inventory from the market, lowering the supply for the existing demand.

Mutual funds accumulate a stock over time, because they want to establish it as a major holding. Large money managers can't buy millions of shares of a stock at one time. Instead, they buy in stages so they don't push the price up too fast and make it too expensive to accumulate. They will use dips in prices to add to their holdings. One key level is the 50 day SMA for growth stocks in uptrends. Much of the support for stocks at key moving averages is caused by money managers adding to their long term positions by buying at 50 day SMA pullbacks.

Accumulation is when assets are bought as long term holdings or investments and held, creating long term trends of higher highs and higher lows. It is difficult to short markets under accumulation because the pullbacks are very short and buyers are waiting to get in at any pullback. It is easier to go with the flow of the capital into the market than to fight against it; trading the short side and betting on a reversal at an early stage, is a tough one to win. This differs from a market that is being traded, creating resistance where the market runs out of buyers at a specific price range, and then has support at a level where it runs out of sellers at low prices.

The distribution of a market is the opposite of accumulation. This is what causes a long term downtrend. Holders of an asset want out. Big money managers and investors start selling their holdings slowly so they don't push the price down too fast. In a market or stock under distribution, price consistently makes lower highs and lower lows, as sellers overwhelm buyers and keep lowering their prices to find new ones. As key support levels are broken, stop losses are triggered causing more selling and even lower prices.

Dip buyers become overwhelmed with sellers forcing prices lower and short sellers start stepping in to add to the pressure of selling. Downtrending markets tend to be more volatile than uptrending ones, as short covering rallies happen at oversold levels, and dip buyers come back in looking to catch the bottom.

Markets under distribution tend to see selling into the rallies and then the downtrend resumes. In downtrends, it is possible to catch some reversals and reversions back to a previous support level, but trying to buy during a downtrend should be for quick trades, because you're going against the longer term trend and flow of capital out of a market.

Markets need accumulation for long term uptrends and distribution for long term downtrends. Price ranges occur when a market is being traded, and the current holders and active traders have established limits in prices on where they will buy and sell. Long term, the stock market has a bullish slant because it has demand from buyers of mutual funds, retirement accounts, company buybacks, and investors. In any market you trade, you should look for clues as to whether it is being accumulated or distributed, or just traded actively by the majority of participants. Make a habit of trading on the side of the flow of capital into or out of your market of choice, instead of resisting the reality of price action.

6. The more times a support or resistance level is tested, the greater the odds that it will be broken. Old resistance can become the new support, and the old support may become the new resistance.

What causes price resistance and support on charts? Price has memory. If price makes a new high, then reverses and goes lower, many people left holding a stock at lower prices will decide that if the stock returns to that price level, they will sell it immediately. These holders create a group of sellers waiting for the old price high to be their sell target. When price returns to the old, higher price level, these holders sell and feel relieved. They're happy that they didn't miss their second opportunity to get out at the higher price. This selling sends the price back down again.

A similar thing happens to create a price support level. A group of people want to buy a stock for $98, and when the price pulls back briefly to a price level like $100, then moves up to $105, those that wanted to buy cheap, missed the first opportunity. Frustrated, they decide that if it pulls back to $100 again they will buy at that price. This creates willing buyers at the new support level, just waiting for the opportunity to get in. This is what causes key support and resistance levels for stocks; the memories and goals of the market participants.

Support and resistance levels can play out over and over again, until a breakout happens to a new trading range for prices, or the market begins to be accumulated or distributed. This creates a trend that overwhelms the active traders, and the long term holders take over by building positions or distributing, creating a new trend of consistently higher or lower prices that replaces the old range of set highs and lows.

When a breakout of a trading range occurs and big distributors or accumulators take over a market they cause it to trend, but it doesn't just go straight up or down. There is still a pattern of a market moving in one direction, then meeting supply and demand and retracing. If a stock had an old $105 resistance level and it suddenly breaks out to $108, the odds are good that it will return at least one more time to $105. It will find buyers at that price who wanted to buy the breakout over $105, but they missed the original opportunity. Given a second chance, they will buy a pullback to the breakout level of $105. When they do, this creates support, so old resistance becomes new support in an uptrend. Momentum and trend traders that missed the initial breakout buy the first pullback for an opportunity to get aboard a new trend, in a new higher trading range.

Old support works the same way because holders become trapped in a position as the old support level is lost. They decide that given another opportunity, they will get out if price rallies back to old support. This creates selling pressure because holders of a stock that lost money are looking for a rally to get out when the price returns to the old support level.

The more times resistance and supports are tested, the greater the odds that they will break into a trend as the market works through the current holders of a stock, and new people enter the stock. Make a habit identifying old support and resistance levels and trading off them as long as they hold in a range bound market, then look at trading a breakout.

7. Moving averages can quantify trends and create signals for entries, exits, and trailing stops.

Moving averages on charts is the quickest way to quantify the direction of a trend in any time frame. Moving averages smooth out the price action in a trend, and show what side of the average price is on in any time frame. The slope and direction of the moving average shows the direction and the power of price action.

If price is currently above the 5 day moving average, then a trader knows that the price is going higher in the 5 day time frame. The easiest way to identify a trend is to look for the uptrend as higher highs and higher lows, and the downtrend as lower highs and lower lows. A quick way to identify a trend is to look at the price action versus the moving average in your trading time frame. Price above the key moving average shows an uptrend and price below it shows a downtrend.

I like to use moving averages for trend identification over trend lines and price patterns because they are 100% quantifiable. A moving average is math. You can choose a faster one on a lower time frame like the 10 day SMA, or a slower one on a longer time frame like the 200 day SMA. You can have one that changes fast by giving more weight to newer prices by using an exponential moving average, or one that is an average of prices over a time period with an SMA.

While moving averages aren't the Holy Grail of signals, they can play a very important role in your trading system. They can be backtested on historical data used as trading signals, or used on historical charts to study how price reacted around them. Moving averages can also be used in pairs to create entry and exit signals when a short term moving average crosses a long term one.

Moving averages can be used as entry signals when price breaks above them, or stop losses when price breaks below them. They can be used as trailing stops as you let a winning trade run, and they are trend identification tools that work best when combined with other technical indicators. Moving averages can outperform most people's opinions because they follow price action instead of prediction.

All of the best traders I know have trading rules for moving averages, and utilize them to some extent in their trading systems. I strongly urge you to make a habit of studying moving average systems, backtesting them, and using them on your charts to see what is happening in the market you're trading.

There is a lot more to learn about moving averages, but I won't go into greater detail here, because I have written another book dedicated to these signals.

Moving Averages 101: Incredible Signals that will Make You Money in the Stock Market

8. Bull markets have no long term resistance, and bear markets have no long term support.

Many sellers and 'weak hands' get washed out of a bearish market after experiencing lower lows over a long period of time. During a 20% drop in prices into a bear market, key support levels are lost repeatedly. Stop losses are triggered, rallies are sold into, and fear slowly takes hold as people see money disappearing from their accounts.

Lower highs and lower lows is the recognizable long term pattern as people pile out of their holdings. A downtrending market is the best way to shake out the most holders, and setup the opportunity for prices to stabilize. Starting a trend back up will alleviate a lot of the selling pressure toward the end of the downtrend. The major change with price action during market corrections and bear markets is that dips stop being bought. They are replaced with further dips in price without buyers causing bounces.

Buying key support levels doesn't work because supports don't hold and are instead breakouts of price ranges to the downside. The odds are on your side to sell strength short in bear markets so you stay on the right side of the trend and flow of capital out of the market. A bearish Stock Market is usually short lived, typically lasting for a year or two. Big rallies in bear markets are caused by short covering rallies to lock in profits after a deep plunge in prices. These are then chased by bottom pickers.

The end of a bear market arrives when selling is finally exhausted. With many longer term position holders left onboard, and with dip buyers becoming the majority of the new holders that got in at much lower prices, these new holders are less apt to be stopped out of their new positions. This is the formation of a new bottom that holds.

Big trends in bull or bear markets are usually followed by a time of price consolidation. Prices stabilize and find new ranges to trade inside of. Support and resistance begins to have meaning again, and the market as a whole starts to go sideways, with neither a big return nor loss in the stock market indexes. This is the time period of neutrality and uncertainty. Traders and investors don't know if the last trend is over or whether it will resume. This is a market is traded back and forth without accumulation or distribution to create trends.

The primary characteristic of a bull market is the ability to repeatedly breakout to new highs. First, with a 52 week high, and then all-time highs. Short sellers get hurt during bullish conditions because resistance no longer holds back the advancing prices. As resistance is broken again and again, short sellers are forced to cover. This sets off more momentum, which in turn draws in the momentum traders to buy the strength.

In bull markets, buying is eventually rewarded. Buying dips gives traders and investors the chance to catch the next trip to all-time highs. Being stubborn with long positions is rewarded in the end. Bull markets usually last for several years and are the source of most of the capital appreciation for the long term returns. Learning to get out of investments at the end of a big bull run will dramatically improve the returns of long term buy and hold investors. Traders who switch from buying price strength in stocks, to shorting them in downtrends, will significantly improve their returns.

Having trading rules that identify price patterns for range bound markets, uptrends, and downtrends so you can trade according to the environment will improve your profitability.

9. The larger the market gaps, the greater the odds of continuation and a trend. – Linda Raschke

Price gaps on a chart are generally trend indicators in the direction of the gap. This is especially true for growth stocks and commodities. Most gaps are filled, but it can take months or even a year to fill a gap. You can catch a nice trend in the meantime if the gap turns out to be a "gap and go" that leads to a trend over days, weeks, or months.

A "gap and go" means that the low of the day of the gap holds and a trend sets in over the next few days. When gaps in price fail and move back to fill the gap in price on the day of the gap, they can be called a "gap and crap". If gaps don't fill in the first hour of trading, the odds are that they aren't going to fill, and price will continue in the direction of the gap for the remainder of the day.

The best way to trade a gap is to buy the first pullback to the low of the gap day. This gives you a better risk/return ratio on entry, but the downside is sometimes gaps are so powerful they don't retrace. You can buy into the gap in the morning, but there is more risk because you don't know if the gap will hold. You can also buy the gap at the end of the day with your stop as a close below the low of the gap up day. This is a trade based on the probability of strong momentum and a trend continuation.

There are few things as bullish as a gap up or as bearish as a gap down. This is a strong signal and is not to be ignored. The odds aren't good to bet against the direction. Be aware that gaps at open have overcome the entire string of bid and asks for an entire range of prices, and it's important to listen to what this is telling you.

The location of a gap and go should also be considered. A gap up in the $SPY ETF out of a downtrend from an oversold 30 RSI to a 40 RSI level, will have better odds of trending than a gap up in $SPY late in an uptrend from a 60 RSI to a 70 RSI into overbought territory.

The RSI (Relative Strength Index) in the $SPY typically ranges from a low of 30 oversold, to a high of 70 overbought. A growth stock gapping down to the 200 day moving average will likely find buyers to support it, as selling has become overdone. Gaps late into a long trend can signal the end of a trend. These are called exhaustion gaps and usually occur on large volume, ending the day much lower than the opening price or the high of the day.

Commodities and growth stocks can go farther and trend more than stock indexes or big cap stocks, so gaps in trending types of markets should be respected even more. Traders should have solid rules about trading gaps in the markets on their watch list. Finding a successful way to trade gaps can be very profitable.

10. The last hour often tells the truth about how strong a trend truly is. "Smart" money shows their hand in the last hour, continuing to mark positions in their favor. As long as a market is having consecutive strong closes, look for an up-trend to continue. The uptrend is most likely to end when there is a morning rally first, followed by a weak close. – Linda Raschke

In the stock market, the first hour of trading is often times amateur hour, while the closing hour is like a lie detector.

New traders are lured into taking the wrong side of trades at the open, but most of the smart money waits to see how the market closes before making a decision. In bear markets, the market tends to open higher on the hope of a reversal of the downtrend, and then close lower on distribution when it doesn't occur during the trading day. In a bull market, the market usually tends to open low and go lower on profit taking, closing higher on accumulation.

In my experience, traders would be better served by getting into the habit of taking profits in the morning, and making entry decisions based on the last 30 minutes of the trading day. The morning price action often reverses, and the end of day entries give a clear picture of what happened in the context of the full trading day.

End of day trading is also better psychologically because you avoid the intra-day noise of day traders and automated algorithms battling it out. You get a better perspective of the longer term accumulation and distribution of the large money managers in the market. End of day trading was the primary method that Nicolas Darvas, Ed Seykota, and Tom Basso used to build their wealth

End of day is the time when many trend followers take their own signals. You can also consider whether you take profits at the open, entries at the close, or trade end of day only. Get in the habit of trading your time frame in a disciplined manner, whatever strategy you choose.

11. Above the 200 day is where bulls create uptrends. Bad things happen below the 200 day; downtrends, distribution, bear markets, crashes, and bankruptcies.

The ultimate line in the sand that separates a long term uptrend from a long term downtrend, and a bull market from a bear market, is the 200 day SMA on the daily chart. For long term trend followers that look at higher time frames, a similar line to watch would be the 40 week moving average on the weekly chart.

While many professional traders and investors watch this line and initiate selling and buying as price approaches it, there is nothing inherently magical about the 200 day. What it does is identify the fact that price is trading above or below its average for the past 200 days. This is an effective way to quantify its longer term trend.

For a market to drop 20% into a bear market, or 'meltdown', or 'crash' it will typically first fall through its 200 day moving average. The 200 day is a trend trader's first warning sign that the trend has changed. Buy and hold investors can reduce their drawdowns in trading capital if they exit their long positions when price closes below this line.

Traders can improve their trading win rate by looking for short side trades when price closes below the 200 day, and fails to rally and close back over this line. Price usually finds support on the first few trips to the 200 day, and bulls look to buy this dip for an initial bounce and a great risk/reward ratio. In a young bull market, this is generally the early support line. Later in a bull market when the 200 day is lost, price will tend to rally back over this line.

For stocks that lose this line and begin downtrends, they will often rally back to the 200 day repeatedly, before further distribution takes over and the stock plunges. The 200 day is a way to quantify a long term uptrend from a long term downtrend. The odds are better for long positions in markets above this line and selling short below this line.

The 200 day can be used as a trading system filter, acting as another qualifier before taking entry signals. $SPY breaks over the 50 RSI AND price is over the 200 day, for example. Traders should get in the habit of thinking about going long above the 200 day, and selling short below it in most cases. Waiting for stock index prices to start closing back over the 200 day can be a key level for investors to get back in after a prolonged bear market. This is be the first sign of a new bull market.

12. It is much easier to watch a few than many. – Jesse Livermore

The best way to develop a strong edge in trading is to study, test, trade, and master a specific thing. It is hard to beat an expert in a specific market, setup, chart pattern, trading system, or stock. You will have a much better chance if you have a small watch list of specific stocks or setups.

Knowing how your stocks move around key moving averages and indicators can give you an edge over others that are trading their opinions. Studying how your specific market moved around key technical indicators over the past ten years should provide you with the necessary insight.

Develop a robust system for trading price action across multiple markets. This simply a matter of finding the entry signals and patterns you're looking for that will give you more trading options if your smaller watch list dries up. Get in the habit of trading a specific winning price action based system, so that your trading becomes a simple search for the right signals.

13. Trends never turn on a dime. Reversals build slowly. The first sharp dip always finds buyers and the first sharp rise always finds sellers. – Alan Farley

It is important for traders to understand that trends don't go straight up or straight down. Instead, they tend to zigzag back and forth from a new high, back to a lower high, to a higher high, and back down.

Markets and stocks rarely plunge straight down day after day, or go straight up in price. Even the strongest uptrends in stocks and markets tend to pull back to the 5 day exponential moving average repeatedly on their way to new highs.

Downtrending stock indexes usually bounce a few times at the 30 RSI before continuing lower. Bear markets almost always have strong rallies back to key moving averages like the 200 day SMA before they finally roll over and drop for multiple days in a row. It is important to step back from your daily trading and get a perspective of the daily chart's longer term trend. You have to find good key price levels to enter where you can position your stops to not be hit before you're able to capture a piece of the larger market trend.

In stock indexes, downtrends tend to bounce near the 30 RSI, while uptrends tend to stall near the 70 RSI. The MACD (Moving average convergence divergence) technical indicator attempts to measure a change in trend, and signal a possible entry at the beginning of a new short term trend. A trader can decide how much of a trend they want to try to capture in their chosen time frame, and how much of a profit giveback they are willing to risk to capture more of a trend.

Traders should get in the habit of finding ways to capture trends as the price zigzags and then continues in the primary market direction. Ability to filter out noise and capture a trend is a trader's primary responsibility during system development.

14. Successful trading is about consistently doing the difficult thing so often that it becomes second nature. – Richard Weissman

The easy trade is usually the losing trade. When a trader feels the most comfortable entering a trade to get onboard a trend, it is usually close to the end. It's difficult to take entry signals with great risk/reward ratios because of deep dips in price. This is typically due to fear in the market.

The best dip buying opportunities happen at key support levels due to extreme fear of an event, which triggers a plunge in prices. The vast majority of the time, the feared event doesn't happen and a large rally occurs when the end of the world is avoided.

Traders and investors often say they want to buy a key support level or big pullback, and even have a specific price target, but often times the pullback and dip occurs due to market fears. The potential dip buyer gets so consumed by fear that they can't take their desired entry signal because their emotions take over.

Maximum buying opportunities happen at the height of these false fears that have little basis in reality of the future price. Of course, fear is not a signal in itself. Fear is what creates trading signals as price reaches extreme oversold levels, key long term moving averages, and old price support zones.

Another difficult entry to take is to buy a breakout to new highs out of a price range. The initial breakout over resistance will feel like you're buying too high, chasing, or buying late. A trend up to new all-time highs can only happen after a breakout to a new price level. Momentum traders and trend followers' best trades are usually those that are entered at an initial breakout into a new price zone, and then trend over weeks and months to higher highs or lower lows for days, weeks, or months.

The two most profitable ways to trade are to buy extreme lows that are caused by unfounded fears, or to buy breakouts or momentum at the beginning of a large trend, riding it to big profits. Both are difficult to do because a trader must overcome their own fear.

All the things that make a trader profitable are difficult to do. Buy initial strength, short initial weakness, buy breakouts, sell breakdowns short, and let a winner run with a trailing stop loss, cut a loser short and accept when you're wrong.

Financial markets can be counter intuitive because when things appear to be the most obvious, that is typically when the opportunity has passed. Opportunity exists in a state of uncertainty, when the majority is waiting to see what will happen, and where price will go next. Price will generally go in the direction that causes the most financial and emotional pain to the majority, because the majority is usually wrong over the long term.

15. The best trades work almost right away. – ArtOfTrading.net

The best trades are the ones that fit your entry signal parameters, and have a stop loss at a price level that is unlikely to be hit before the trade is successful The best trades are those that you fully understand and accept the risk/return potential. When your position size is setup so that the stop loss placement limits the size of your potential loss, it is a good trade out of the gate. But the best trades are those that immediately go in your favor, because your entry was at the right moment.

There is little stress associated with these trades because it is immediately profitable, and your stop loss is safe from the start. You realize quickly that this will be a winning trade, and your focus shifts from if it will be successful, to how to manage your winner. Your time and energy will be spent on how and when to exit the trade to lock in your profits.

The odds of having a winning trade from the beginning increases if you wait for an initial move in the direction you want to enter, instead of stepping in to catch a falling knife, or sell a rocket short that is blasting upwards

Mind Over Emotion

16. Wishful thinking must be banished. – Jesse Livermore

Hope is a dangerous emotion in the stock market. Hope for a big winning trade causes people to take position sizes that are too large, and opens them up to even bigger losses. The misplaced hope of a loss becoming profitable, leads some traders to ignore their initial stop loss and stay positioned on the wrong side of a trend for far too long.

The stronger the hope of turning a small account into a big account, the greater the chance that a trader engages in risky trades and takes their small account to zero. Hope is a powerful tool when it fuels a trader's passion to learn, study, and grow with patience and perseverance. However, hope isn't a trading plan, it isn't a signal, and isn't a guide on what to do.

When it comes to making decisions about your trading account, traders must get in the habit of trading hope for facts and emotions for trading rules. Hope is a great tool for personal goal setting, but a terrible guide when making trading decisions.

17. Money is made by discounting the obvious and betting on the unexpected. – George Soros

The obvious trades that everyone thinks are a no-brainer, usually don't work because when a trade becomes obvious, it's too late. As the winning traders prepare their exit strategies to lock in profits, the unprofitable traders are preparing for their entries to chase a late trend.

The unexpected happens regularly as growth stocks go higher than anyone believed possible, but the early buyers and bear markets go deeper than expected because fear of loss begins overriding any fundamental valuation. When everyone agrees with your long trade, beware. Who is left to buy?

If everyone thinks you're nuts for buying a deep dip in price because the world could end, then most of the selling pressure should already be gone, and a market should be due for a rally. The "everyone hates your trade indicator" is a good because it shows that the majority has already made their move, and you're the first to spot a new trend or reversal.

Extremes in sentiment are a sign that the majority have already made their move and a new move could be near. Obvious or unexpected aren't trading signals, so you need to look for technical signals that line up with the extreme market sentiment.

Get in the habit of being the contrarian. When the majority thinks that a trend has to stop immediately, or that it will go on forever, you need to beware. Trade your best signals when the majority thinks you're crazy.

18. A losing trade costs you money, but letting a losing trade get too far out of hand can cause you to lose your nerve. Cut losses for the sake of your nerves and your capital.

A trader can come back after losing money, losses happen. A lot of great traders came back, even after losing entire trading accounts. It's much more difficult for a trader to come back after they lose their confidence.

A terrible use of time and energy is letting a trade go against you, through your stop loss, then holding it as it gets bigger and bigger. Spending a day sweating and stressing over a losing trade hoping it will come back, is time wasted. It is always better to take your loss where you planned and move on with your life.

Letting a small loss turn into a big loss is expensive both financially and emotionally. If you want to be a trader for the long haul, it's crucial that you always take the small loss where you planned for the sake of stress management. There are more productive ways a trader can spend their time than watching every tick of the price, and praying that it reverses so they can get back out.

Get in the habit of taking your initial stop loss to limit loss of your mental capital and your most valuable asset, time.

19. Never trade position sizes so large that your emotions take over your trading plan.

You have to trade with a position size that you can handle, both mentally and emotionally. Many traders have to build up larger position sizes over a period of time, because the stress of trading and risking their capital creates unpleasant reactions. You have to trade with a position size that keeps your emotions and ego in check.

The moment you start having trouble following your trading plan because you don't want to take a loss, or admit you're wrong and exit, you have entered a danger zone. Your trading should be conducted like a business. When you have an accelerated heart beat and sweaty palms, then something has gone wrong.

Lower your position size so a win is still meaningful but you can trade in an unemotional state. Don't trade 500 shares of a stock that you should only be trading 100 shares of. Most traders have no problem losing $50 or $100, but the idea of losing $500, $1000, or more makes them physically ill.

You can't trade with a position size that impedes your ability to follow your trading plan. Find the size that removes the emotional dynamic from your trading. If 500 shares stress you, go down to 300 or less until you can trade in a relaxed state. Remember that each trade is just one of your next 100. It is just a trade.

Get in the habit of trading a position size that keeps you emotionally neutral.

20. Trade the market, not the money. – Richard Weissman

Trading decisions should be made based on price action and not the need to make money. A stop loss must be based on the price level that you're proven wrong, not at the level where you have lost all the money you can stand to lose.

Profit targets have to be set at technical levels of price resistance, and not on your own profit target. Trade based on your actual trading system, rather than the amount lost or gained on a trade. You don't exit a trade because you have lost over $100; you exit a trade because your stop loss was hit. You don't set your stop loss arbitrarily at a 1% loss of your total trading capital; you find the price level that will show you that your trade is wrong, and position size so that your maximum loss would be 1% of your total trading capital.

Professionals in other fields don't stop and calculate the money that they have made in the middle of the day; they are too busy focusing on process.

Get in the habit of focusing on your trading system and following the process for entries, exits, and position size, rather than the money you are making or losing at any particular moment.

21. When there's nothing to do, do nothing. – Richard Weissman

Traders lose money by entering trades they shouldn't due to boredom or because they're trying to make something happen. The motivation for taking a trade should be a good signal with a good risk/reward ratio and probability of success.

Bad trades are usually because a trader is impatient and wants to make money as quickly as possible. Losing trades happen when a good entry signal leads to your stop loss being hit, while a bad trade is one that you shouldn't be in to begin with. The ability to stop making bad trades can benefit the trader as much as taking the good trades.

A trader has to allow themselves to be bored and wait for just the right moment. Being early to a trade can cost you money, because you're front running a signal that may never happen. It's also dangerous to chase a trade late in a move, because the risk/reward ratio will not be as favorable as a trend advances.

The ability to do nothing unless there is a signal is a powerful and profitable habit to develop. Self-control, patience, and impulse control will save you a lot of time, money, and sanity.

22. Trade what's happening...not what you think is gonna happen. – Doug Gregory

There is a big difference between predictive technical analysis and reactive technical analysis. Predicting is trying to forecast where prices will go in the future and taking trades based on that belief. Reactive trading is based on taking a trade after a signal has indicated the beginning of a trend.

It is predictive to believe that the stock market is coming out of a bear market and buy based on that belief. It is reactive trading to plan to buy into the stock market when a key index breaks over and closes above the 200 day moving average, because this is the first indication that the market is coming out of the bear market.

The biggest leap to profitability comes when we stop taking trades based on what we think should happen in the market, and instead learn to trade signals that react to what is happening. Chart patterns, moving averages, and breakouts of ranges are designed to capture trends based on signals.

You should trade quantitative signals that give you good probabilities of capturing a trend in your timeframe. The market doesn't care about your opinion. It will go where it wants to go based on all of the participants' actions.

Get in the habit of going with the flow, and avoid trying to predict where the flow is going.

23. Develop systems based on the kinds of "pain" (weaknesses) endured when they aren't working or you'll abandon them during drawdowns. – Richard Weissman

One of the most important questions a trader can ask before they start trading is how much of a drawdown in capital they can endure before quitting. If you start with $100,000 in trading capital, will you stop trading your system after you're down 10%? Is $90,000 the most pain you can handle in a drawdown before you quit? Can you keep trading at $85,000 or $80,000? This is a crucial question that must be answered before you begin your trading journey.

Structure your trading so you have a low probability of being broken by a single drawdown. Traders have to set parameters for their returns, targeting 20% annual returns with max drawdowns of 5%, for example. More aggressive goals might be 30% annual returns with 10% maximum drawdowns. The aggressiveness of your returns will be correlated with your drawdowns. The bigger your desired return, the more you have to risk, and the greater the chance of experiencing a drawdown during losing streaks.

Your system design for winning percentage and risk exposure should be created with your risk tolerance and return goals in mind. If you want your max drawdown from an equity high to be 5%, your risk per trade needs to be ½% to 1% per trade. Your system's winning percentage should be high enough so that several losers in a row won't give you more than a 5% drawdown.

A drawdown is based on any new equity high. If you go from $100,000 to $110,000 and back to $99,000, that is a 10% drawdown from a new equity high, even though it is only a 1% drawdown from the original starting equity of $100,000. Many traders make the mistake of gambling with profits from their starting equity because they think of it as 'the house's money'. Profits are yours once they go into your account, and if you want to keep them, you will need to treat them with the same care as the money you started with.

Get in the habit of remembering the maximum drawdown in trading capital that you can mentally and emotionally endure, and design your trading system with position sizing and risk exposure in a way that you never reach your breaking point.

24. Remain flexible and go with the flow of the market price action. Stubbornness, egos, and emotions are the worst indicators for entries and exits.

Emotions and egos are the worst trading signals. The majority of market participants operate based on their feelings rather than identifying the trend in a market. You should focus on finding the trend, and then trading in the direction of its accumulation or distribution. This will give you a substantial edge over other, less disciplined market participants.

When your competition is selling late in a downtrend because they fear losing money, you can buy with a great risk/reward ratio. When people are afraid to buy a breakout of a price base to all-time highs, you can take the momentum signal to buy high and sell higher.

Downtrends, uptrends, and range bound markets have different characteristics, and successful traders identify what kind of market they are in and trade the price action as it unfolds.

Get in the habit of taking good signals based on price action, and leave your opinions and predictions at the door.

25. A trader can only be successful after they have faith in themselves as a trader, their trading system as a winner, and know that they will remain disciplined.

Faith in yourself will come after you have done your homework, and you have proven that you can be trusted to follow your trading plan with discipline. The biggest reason new traders tend to fail in their first year, is that they put confidence in their trading abilities before they have any competence in trading.

Faith in yourself as a trader is crucial for your success, but it has to be warranted faith. You must have a trading system with an edge, you must manage your risk, and you must have the self-control to avoid blowing up your account. Above all else, when you learn what to do in a given situation, you must trust yourself to do the right things in the heat of trading.

Without confidence, you will be unable to enter trades effectively, but with too much confidence, you will trade too big and destroy yourself. Have faith in yourself that you will not only do the right things, but you will also avoid the wrong things.

26. One thing I have learned over the years trading is that crisis = opportunity. – Dean Karrys

The strongest downtrends that short sellers love, usually come during a perceived crisis. The deep dips that traders buy during bull markets, where the stock indexes drop to near the 30 RSI or 200 day moving average, typically occur in an environment of maximum fear.

The best margin of safety for value investors looking to buy into individual stocks at great valuations usually occur during a crisis in the market. They can also happen at the individual company that creates a steep drop in price based on fear of loss, rather than fundamental valuations.

The opportunity that comes from a crisis is to sell short early, buy the fear later, and sell the relief rally when the world doesn't end. But you can't just buy into a crisis. You have to wait for the crisis to cause the right signals that tell you to buy or sell short. Your signals must be based off reactive technical analysis, past support and resistance levels, chart pattern confirmation, and technical tools like the MACD, RSI, and key moving averages.

Look for opportunity in every crisis. Ask yourself where the best risk/reward ratios lie in selling short, buying the deep dip, and trading reversals and gaps.

Get in the habit of developing your own reactive technical trading signals and trade them with discipline.

27. Going up on bad news or down on good news are among the strongest market tells. – Richard Weissman

If unexpected bad news can't take a market uptrend down, then what can? What can send a downtrending market back up, if not unexpected good news? It is bullish when markets go up on bad news, and bearish when a market goes down on good news. It shows that the market participants are staying with a trend, even with news that goes against their positions. This is a filter to consider when using a discretionary trading system.

Get in the habit of watching how the market reacts to news that is counter to the existing trend. News itself is not a signal, but it can be combined with a trading signal to reinforce a trade's viability. If $SPY rallied off the 30 RSI on bad news inside a long term uptrend over the 200 day, it would reinforce the trade setup and give more confidence of a sustained bounce.

Rule 28 – 39

The Keys to Profitability

28. Manage losses and maximize gains.

All your trades should end in one of four ways: a small win, a big win, a small loss, or break even. You should never experience a big loss. If you can get rid of big losses, you have a great chance of being profitable for years to come.
Traders just starting out often discover that big losses are the one thing that hurt their overall long term returns the most. If those few big losses were removed, their returns would go up dramatically. The fastest way to improve your trading returns is to immediately stop having the few big losses that force you to give back weeks, and sometimes months of winning trading profits.

The use of a stop loss on every trade is the one thing that can stop you from having huge losses. A stop loss is the cost of insurance you pay to avoid being caught on the wrong side of a large market trend. It may be frustrating to have a small loss, then the market reverses and goes in your direction. However, it is still better to insure that you have a small loss than risk a big one.

Stop losses should be placed at a price level that will not be easily reached unless your trade is not going to work out. Stop losses should be placed outside the range of normal price action and out of the reach of 'noise'. When you enter a discretionary trade, find the spot where you say "If price gets to this level, then I am probably wrong about the direction."

Trailing stops help you maximize gains by raising your stops as a winning trade trends in your direction. In strong trends, the 5 day EMA or 10 day SMA can be an excellent end of day stop if price closes below these levels.

Get in the habit of knowing where your stop loss will be before you enter a trade. Small losses is one of the primary ways to experience profitable trading.

29. The key to long-term survival and prosperity has a lot to do with the money management techniques incorporated into the technical system. – Ed Seykota

It is position sizing, and not the brilliance of entries and exits, that will ultimately determine a trader's long term profitability, total risk exposure at one time, and their exposure to the risk of ruin during a losing streak. The quickest and easiest way to answer how good the parameters of your money management system are, will be to figure out how many losing trades you can have in a row and survive.

Regardless of what you perceive your winning percentage will be, reality could be more painful than expected. A 50% drawdown in capital is difficult to recover from because it will take a 100% return just to get back to even. And the odds are that if your system is bad enough to allow for a 50% drawdown, then you will be at zero before you can recover.

Your success as a trader will largely be based on your ability to either have a low winning percentage with big wins and small losses, or a high winning percentage with small wins and small losses.

Having a money management system that continuously exposes your capital to the risk of large losses will catch up with you at some point, regardless of your previous winning streaks.

30. Be disciplined in risk management and flexible in perceiving market behavior. – Richard Weissman

While trading price action requires an open mind and the flexibility to adjust to what is happening, risk management is a strict discipline of doing what you planned to do, without deviation.

Once a stop loss is chosen, it must be set in stone. It can be deadly to your account to decide not to take your initial stop loss when it's triggered. This is especially true in growth stocks, because once they are under distribution, their plunge can be devastating to traders on the wrong side of the move.

When a well-placed stop loss is triggered, it may mean that a breakdown is underway, and you're on the wrong side of a parabolic move against your position. Stop loss set at a close below the 30 RSI or the 200 day moving average is a low probability event inside a bull market uptrend, but once these levels are closed below, it should set off signs of a parabolic move down as these key levels are lost.

Develop the habit of not arguing, bargaining, or hoping once your stop loss is triggered. Get out of the trade, because your long term profitability depends on it. Once you have set a quality stop loss with a low probability of being reached, you must take it.

31. Position sizing can be correlated to the quality of a trade setup.

Regardless of setup, it is important to have different position size parameters based on the quality of your entry and the risk/reward parameters. It is a better strategy to risk your maximum position size on your best setups, and your smallest position size on your less likely trades.

All long term traders should have some top notch trade setups that have the highest probability of success. Those are the trades they should enter with their maximum size, because they are pretty rare. The trader can also have a normal trade size that is commonly used day to day on other high probability setups.

Then move on to the smallest position size for entries that meet your parameters, but could be the first signal out of a period of a trading range or volatility, and that may not work the first time around.

I know traders that have gotten into the habit of swinging the hardest at the fat pitches that are over the plate, and they have substantially increased their returns by doing so.

Get in the habit of making your best trades be your biggest trades, and your losing trades the smallest. Mastering this strategy will dramatically improve your performance.

32. Never lose more than 1% of your total trading capital on any one trade.

The one percent rule is something that new traders struggle to understand, but it is one of the most important dynamics of active trading. The 1% rule does not mean only trading with 1% of your trading capital, and it doesn't mean only risking 1% of the stock you're trading.

If you're trading a $100,000 account, then no losing trade should ever be over $1,000. This means that if you trade 500 shares of Apple, with a $100,000 account, you can only risk $2 on this trade, because if Apple drops $2 and you own 500 shares, you will lose $1,000. This is a simplified example, but it illustrates the principle.

The 1% rule means you never lose more than 1% of your total trading account on any one losing trade, through the use of proper position sizing based on the right technical stop loss level for trading a particular stock or index.

If you make the 1% rule one of your trading habits, each trade will mathematically be 1 of the next 100 trades. It is hard to have a large drawdown in capital if a five trade losing streak results in 5% drawdown in trading capital. For bigger accounts, 1% may be too much risk per trade. If you think the rule is too strict, then your account size may well be the issue, rather than the principle.

Many of the best traders believe in and practice this rule, and it makes their trading careers long and profitable. With this rule, you don't have to fear big drawdowns or account blowups. It will remove the emotional rollercoaster from your trading, and turn it into a business. Rich traders use the 1% rule to become rich, because they never blew up their account, and even in unpleasant market conditions, they survived to trade another day.

33. First find the right stop loss level that will show you that you're wrong about a trade, then set your positions size based on that price level.

If you buy 500 shares of Apple at $120, and the key support level is at $118 near the 200 day moving average, then the 1% rule makes sense. However, this rule is not to be used solely for placing stop losses. You must first find the price level of support or resistance that should hold if your trade is going to work, and then position size based on the 1% rule.

If your stop loss needs to be $5 under the current Apple price, close to the 200 day moving average instead of the previous example, then you could only trade 200 shares of Apple at $120. You will bring your mathematical risk of ruin as close to zero as possible with the 1% rule. You don't want your stop to be too tight; stop losses in obvious places tend to be taken out. It is better not to set a hard stop with your broker exactly at the 200 day.

I personally use end of day stops and smaller position sizes to avoid the majority of the intra-day noise and keep from being stopped out prematurely. You should set a stop loss a little beyond a moving average like 1% below, or as an end of day stop to avoid having your stop triggered before the reversal in your favor.

Get in the habit of setting stop losses just a little beyond the most obvious support or resistance levels to avoid being stopped out prematurely, and only when you're definitely wrong. Even with end of day stops, I step in and take my loss if I am down over 1% in total trading capital at any point intraday. That is rare with my position sizing and stop levels based on the current volatility.

34. Never lose more than 3% of your total trading capital on your worst day.

I recommend that you never have more than three trades open at any one time, risking no more than 1% on each. You're relatively safe if on your worst day, when all your trades go against you, you're only down 3%. At that point, you still have the opportunity to capture a market trend.

3% should be your maximum risk exposure when all your signals line up. During volatile or directionless markets, you can also have 0% risk exposure. This gives you flexibility with how much risk you want, and when you want it. It also limits the drawdowns that many investors see in bear markets, because a trader doesn't have a portfolio of investments, they have a few trades on at a time.

Get in the habit of limiting your total capital at risk exposure to a maximum of 3% at any one time and you will avoid big, one day disasters when everything goes against you.

35. When I am trading poorly, I keep reducing my position size. That way, I will be trading my smallest position size when my trading is worst. – Paul Tudor Jones

The worse you're trading, the smaller your trades should be. Conversely, you should be at your maximum position size during winning streaks. Traders usually have losing streaks because the market environment has changed its nature from volatile to not volatile, from an uptrend to a downtrend, or from a trend to range bound.

Analyze a losing streak or a winning streak to help you understand the type of market you're currently trading. To maximize your current opportunity or minimize your potential for more losses, adjust your position sizing and total risk exposure.

Get in the habit of being less aggressive when losing, and more aggressive when winning. Let the market tell you when you're right or wrong.

36. Losers average losers.

It is a deadly habit for a trader to average down on a losing trade when they are already proven wrong. Being rewarded for this behavior with a rally will just reinforce the bad habit, and there will come a time when it never recovers and the account is destroyed.

Adding to a losing trade is fighting a trend, not accepting when you're wrong, and tying up capital that could be used to make money on good trades.

Get in the habit of never adding to a losing trade, learning from the experience, and moving on to the next trade.

37. Never allow a statistically significant unrealized gain to turn into a statistically significant realized loss. – Richard Weissman

Once you have a sizeable winning trade, it needs to stay a profitable trade with the use of trailing stop losses or price targets for profit taking. The only way to exit with a profit is to have an exit strategy that enables you to lock in that money while it is still on the table.

There is a window of opportunity for locking in gains, and you have to establish parameters for this because winning trades have shelf lives, and they usually return to where they started. If you're long the $SPY as it approaches the 70 RSI, it's a good time to look at locking in a profit from an uptrend, for example.

If you're long a strong growth stock that has been going up for ten days straight, it fails to make a new high, and is going to close below the 5 day EMA for the first time in ten days, it's time to consider locking in your profits. Many traders focus on the entries, but money is only made on the exits.

Get in the habit of having a plan to lock in profits with a winning trade, and never allow a big winning trade to reverse and turn into a losing trade.

38. Understand the nature of instability and adjust your position size for the increased risk due to volatility spikes.

Know the trading range of your stock or index over the last ten days and position size accordingly. You should be able to handle a 50% increase in a trading range without having a devastating loss.

Get in the habit of position sizing for the worst case scenario, and not the best case scenario, or the status quo. Always manage risk and be ready to adjust quickly when faced with volatile markets.

39. Place your stop losses outside the range of noise so you're only stopped out when you're wrong.

Find the price level for your stop loss that has a high probability of never being hit, so you have the time to exit your trade profitably. Once you know where that level is, you can enter your trade when that level is near, and position size correctly so the worst case scenario is a small loss.

Many traders choose to look for the highest probability setups to take entries, but if your stop loss is a low probability exit, you have a potentially great trade because your stop loss won't be hit, and you can let a winner run.

Get in the habit of finding low probability stop losses as much as high probability setups.

Just like in athletics, business, and entertainment, the top traders have spent thousands of hours developing and successfully implementing their trading plans. What start out as rules are practiced until they become deeper and more meaningful; they become habits.

It takes discipline and perseverance to reach this level of success, but it can be done. And I promise that if you commit yourself to a regimen of daily trading rituals, and practice them faithfully, you will be a better trader.

The purpose of this book is not to make you adopt my trading habits, but to show you the importance of following a plan that will empower your success. I hope that you now feel confident about creating your own habits, and that they help you achieve your trading goals.

Special thanks to Richard Weissman, Dean Karrys, and Doug Gregory for letting us use some of their quotes and rules. They are some of the best, and an inspiration to traders everywhere.

Steve Burns
New Trader U

Be a better trader

In the New Trader 101 e-course, you'll get:

-13 high quality videos covering how and why to trade

-Real trade examples with detailed charts

-An active member forum with hundreds of ongoing conversations

Visit **newtraderu.com** and join other traders just like you!

Did you enjoy this eBook?

Please consider writing a review.

Read more of our bestselling titles:

New Trader 101

Moving Averages 101

85464402R00035